It's a Beautiful Life

Authors

Kelly Tung, Alexa Jordan, Andrea Schmidt, Elise Buellesbach, Emily McElroy, Alia O'Brien, Arjin Claire, Himal Bamzai-Wokhlu, Sophie Meade, Danielle Huli, Emily Sheridan, Jacqueline See-Tho

Table of Contents

Preface

We are Food Allergy Research & Education's (FARE) Teen Advisory Group (TAG) members, and we have written this book named "It's a Beautiful Life" for our 2020 TAG project. "It's a Beautiful Life" is a book full of our individual experiences living with food allergies. It offers encouragement for those managing food allergies, and for those without food allergies, it demonstrates how to show care and empathy. Our project leader is Kelly Tung, and the authors are Kelly Tung, Alexa Jordan, Andrea Schmidt, Elise Buellesbach, Emily McElroy, Alia O'Brien, Arjin Claire, Himal Bamzai-Wokhlu, Sophie Meade, Danielle Huli, Emily Sheridan, and Jacqueline See-Tho.

We would like to give a special thanks to Food Allergy Research & Education (FARE) for their continued support. We would like to recognize Kristi Grim, FARE's Director of National Programs, for providing us constant guidance and support. We also greatly appreciate Janine Guzzone, FARE's Assistant Director of Individual Giving, for guiding us throughout the fundraising process of our project.

Our goal is to share our experiences with others and educate people about how we managed our food allergies. This book encourages people with allergies to stay optimistic about their allergies and empowers them to become advocates of food allergies. Our stories emphasize the importance of empathy and how to be thoughtful towards people with food allergies. We truly want to help raise awareness for allergies, make a change in the allergy community, and help out those with food allergies as much as we can. We will be donating our book revenue to FARE to fund Teen Advisory Group projects, innovation, allergy research, and youth programs.

A Blessing in Disguise

Kelly Tung

Having food allergies can be challenging, but they allow us to find and develop our strengths. My food allergies have made a huge impact on my life. Although they have thrown countless obstacles my way, my food allergies have helped me discover my strengths and allowed me to grow into the person I am today. I want to tell you how having food allergies has made me brave, compassionate, empathetic, caring, strong, confident, responsible, and accountable. This is my journey with food allergies.

My allergies seemed suffocating when I was little. My allergy responses were frightening and I had to be careful whenever I ate. At home, I was constantly reminded by my parents to stay safe and to read food labels. This environment was only worse in the outside world: family friends were too scared to give me food, negligent teachers would refuse to provide snacks for me, and I couldn't even eat the delicious birthday cake at my friends' parties. I could not understand why I had food allergies when many of my friends did not. The negative stigma I had towards allergies only increased with each allergic reaction I endured.

I felt frustrated and bitter whenever my allergies hindered me. I finally gathered the courage to speak up about my allergies in first grade. There was a time when my lunch bag was stolen. I could not eat lunch because I was allergic to all of the meals offered in the cafeteria that day. Later, I spoke with my teacher and we discovered that two of my classmates hid my lunch bag because they knew I had food allergies. My classmates confessed that they thought it was fun to see me hungry and they promised that they would not do that again.

In another incident, when an afterschool teacher repeatedly skipped my snacks, I stood up for myself and reminded her that there were other alternatives that I could eat. Since that single statement, that teacher never skipped my snacks again. I had taken action against the negligence, discrimination, and bullying I faced both in and out of school, and I witnessed my actions making a difference.

After those incidents, I became braver and stronger. I started to stand up for myself and voice my opinions to others. When my friends made hurtful statements about my allergies, I faced them head-on and let them know that they were hurting my feelings. It took a lot of bravery and courage to stand up to my friends, but by doing so, I stopped being teased by them. I also began helping my other friends who had allergies and supported them wholeheartedly when they were bullied by others.

I realized that education played a critical role in preventing my peers from bullying those with food allergies. I discovered that many of my peers did not know what a food allergy was until I defined it for them. I did my best to educate my friends and peers about allergies by inviting them to visit FARE's website and lending them books about food allergies. Once my friends and peers learned about food allergies, they became more empathetic, welcomed inclusivity, and respected diversity. I watched as our school culture around food allergies significantly improved. I realized the importance of raising food allergy awareness and I knew that I made a change in the community.

Having allergies also taught me the importance of empathy. Empathy is the ability to put yourself in other people's shoes and understand their situations, feelings, and challenges. Several of my friends were outcasts because of their food allergies. They shared their experiences with me, describing how they were bullied on the school bus, catcalled by others in the cafeteria, and afraid that others would threaten them with their food allergies. I empathized with their experiences and I put myself in their shoes. A safe learning environment is essential for students. It is imperative for us to raise awareness of food allergies and to create an environment that embraces diversity, differences, and inclusion whilst promoting empathy at the same time.

Having empathy is key for all forms of understanding between different races, genders, ethnicities, and more. My allergies helped me connect with all of these injustices and taught me to fight against them. It is imperative for everyone to understand the importance of empathy and valuing differences.

An essential lesson that I've learned from having allergies is to *never* be a bystander. If you see someone suffering, lend them a hand! Even something as minor as hearing them out and listening to their troubles can make a big difference. I've always put mutual understanding as a top priority with the people around me. Sharing my allergy experiences with others who were going through similar situations ignited the light within me. Listening to others is already a great first step and the next step is to take action.

I closed the first chapter in my book and started on a whole new journey. I wanted to actively fight for change in my school and my community. My food allergies motivated me to advocate for food allergy awareness and education. My first destination was the Food Allergy Research and Education's Teen Summit. In November of 2017, I joined FARE's Teen Summit and I learned about empowerment and advocacy. I made one of the best decisions of my life when I decided to join their Teen Advisory Group. I was in a safe and friendly environment with countless teens that had gone through the same experiences as me. Better yet, we were all headed towards the same goal of raising awareness for and educating others about food allergies!

I attended FARE's Teen Summit in 2017 and I really enjoyed it!

I received so much support from my TAG family and I was given opportunities to lead different projects and help raise the voice of the food allergy community. I led others to create engaging allergy videos and this book is one of the projects that I worked on with other teens! Seeing everyone's efforts blossom into success taught me the importance and happiness that comes with making a positive impact. Since then, I have always strived to educate others about food allergies and how to be empathetic towards people with allergies; how to help people understand the challenges that people with food allergies face; how to encourage people with food allergies to be brave; and, how to improve the quality of life for people with food allergies.

My activism in the food allergy community has helped me build up greater empathy and empowered me to think bigger. I started expanding towards other large issues in the world such as global warming and lack of teen engagement in the community. I understand the challenges that people who have allergies face, and this has motivated me to put effort into researching factors associated with allergies.

I have learned that climate change and pollution not only worsen people's allergies and damage public health, but also hurt our environment. Since then, I've worked for a cleaner and more sustainable environment for my community. I have gotten actively involved in climate and environmental activism, as this not only benefits our environment and our health but also enhances fairness and justice in the climate movement. I participated in the World of 7 Billion Video Contest and won first place in the Preventing Pollution category. I continued my work for the environment by forming a group called the JFK Green Commuters when I was 12 years old to advocate for sustainability in my middle school.

I enjoy volunteering and I want to make our environment cleaner and healthier.

I know that my generation has the power to change the world and make a huge contribution to our communities and our earth. At the age of 15, I founded a nonprofit organization, Youth Environmental Power Initiative, whose aim is to spread awareness of sustainability and environmental justice, promote alternative transportation and safe biking and walking, and lead future leaders to fight against climate change to make positive changes for our environment. We received grant funding from Silicon Valley Clean Energy and are partnered with the City of Cupertino Safe Routes to School program. I also became directly involved with local governments in order to better the quality of life for students in our community. I wanted to advocate for public policy and teen engagement, leading me to become the Chair of the City of Cupertino Teen Commission.

I was the youngest volunteer at Cupertino's Annual Earth Day & Arbor Day Festival in 2018.

My allergies prompted me to realize that many people need our help and compassion. My journey brought me to visit and perform music for seniors at senior centers and senior care facilities. Every time I visit, I am constantly in awe at the amount of joy and love that my simple harmonies bring. The love and care that I put into my songs are always returned in every smile that I receive from the residents. And that is when I realized that life is truly beautiful. The memories that I have experienced make life what it is today.

Although I initially thought that having egg and nut allergies was terrible, when I reflect on my experiences, I realize that these allergies have positively changed my mindset and health. Due to my food allergies, I was not able to a lot of foods as they contained my allergens. However, this motivated me to try out foods with substitutes for my allergens and encouraged me to learn how to cook. I can now cook a variety of delicious meals and I have learned so much about nutrition and food safety. If I did not have food allergies, I probably would not have gained the cooking skills that I now possess. I love cooking and it makes me very happy to see people enjoying the food I make.

I celebrated my birthday with a slice of egg-free cake!

My journey with food allergies has not only transformed me into a strong and powerful person who can stand up for herself, but it has emboldened me on my quest to make a positive impact on the world. The challenges that I have faced have turned into the words of empowerment and inspiration that I speak today. Even some of the allergies that once chained me down no longer bound me. I've outgrown many of my allergies over the course of 15 years, including my egg allergy! Although some of my allergies have faded, the memories and experiences that I've built from them have not. Having food allergies, for me, was truly a blessing in disguise.

About the Author of A Blessing in Disguise

Kelly Tung

Kelly Tung is a sophomore at Monta Vista High School, who joined Food Allergy Research & Education's (FARE) Teen Advisory Group (TAG) in 2018. Since the age of 12, Kelly has worked extensively to serve the community with her leadership skills and advocacy for sustainability, safe walking and biking, inclusion, and food allergy awareness.

Kelly has vast leadership experience, such as being the Chair of the City of Cupertino's Teen Commission, the President and Executive Director of Youth Environmental Power Initiative, the Founder and President of JFK Green Commuters (received a City of Cupertino Sustainability Commission Student Grant), the President of Design Thinking For Teens Silicon Valley Chapter, the

President of the Columbia Business School Venture For All Club @ Kennedy Middle School Division, and the Student Executive Board Member for Walk-Bike Cupertino.

In 2019, Kelly was the leader of FARE's TAG "Be Brave, Be Thoughtful, and Be Kind" project. She led a team of 14 TAG members as they created videos to raise awareness of food allergies. These videos encouraged people to be confident regardless of their food allergies and educated others about how to be thoughtful, empathetic, and considerate towards people with food allergies.

Kelly is honored to lead another TAG project again in 2020. This project is named "It's a Beautiful Life" and includes 23 TAG members, and 12 of these 23 TAG members have combined their experiences into this book. She hopes that this book will encourage people to stay optimistic about their allergies and empower them to advocate for allergy awareness. Kelly believes that her team's stories will inspire other teens and change their lives for the better.

Besides being actively involved in communities, Kelly is also actively involved at school. She is currently on the ASB Student Life Leadership Commission at Monta Vista High School and is in charge of managing school clubs and Legislative Council, with the goal of encouraging and promoting student interests on campus.

Kelly is passionate about design thinking, innovation, political science, and artificial intelligence. She strongly believes that empathy is a core value that helps people build connections with others, encourages people to appreciate differences, promotes positive behaviors, and resolves problems.

Kelly believes that age is just a number and youths have the power to change the world. She hopes that her literary piece will encourage readers to find the "blessing in disguise" in their lives as well.

Converting Adversity into Political Action

Alexa Jordan

I rushed around my dorm room, frantically packing the last few things before I was due to leave for the Boston Logan Airport. My Economics final happened just two days ago, and my goodness, Harvard students know how to party in their time off. With only a limited time for dinner, I was greeted at Annenberg Hall by an array of putrescent food options. I just couldn't stomach any of it, so I was determined that I could find something safe to eat at the airport. As someone who has lived with a severe tree nut allergy their whole life, I am always extremely careful about the food I buy and the food I eat.

By the time I passed through airport security it was almost 8:00 pm, and I was starving. I stood in front of the menu for several minutes reading each ingredient of every wrap and salad from a restaurant in Terminal A. Not a single salad contained nuts and I double-checked with the cashier (who confirmed that the salad was nut-free), so I ordered my Asian salad.

As soon as my salad was prepared, I had to sprint to my gate. I noticed that the employee making my salad did not have gloves on when preparing the food, so alarm bells were already ringing in my head. My flight was going to be boarding soon, so I didn't have any time to worry. I grabbed my salad and hurried to my gate.

I had a few minutes to spare before I needed to take my seat on the plane, so I took off the lid to my salad and ate a tomato. My tongue started tingling very intensely, but I figured I must have just imagined it. After all, the salad didn't have nuts in it! I shut the lid and took my seat on the plane.

During takeoff, I kept the salad below my seat until I just couldn't bear it any longer. I was so hungry, so I gingerly opened the lid and ate one piece of the chicken and lettuce.

To my horror, my throat started tingling, scratching, and then it began to tighten. My stomach started to experience a bursting pain, and I felt like I was going to puke. I was going into anaphylaxis 30,000 feet in the air, all because of cross-contamination (from a cashew nut, I found out later).

I ran to the front of the cabin and asked the Southwest flight attendants if they had any Benadryl - I quickly explained that I have a severe tree nut allergy and that my throat was beginning to shut. After checking with the back of the airplane, they told me that they did not have any. They were automatically flustered and alarmed, unsure of what to do.

My throat was continually closing, and I was getting lightheaded as it became almost impossible to breathe. The flight attendants didn't offer epinephrine, an EpiPen, and they were completely unprepared to help me. The flight attendants did *not* ask the passengers if there was a physician on board, and they did *not* inform me they had any sort of medicine to help me.

I told them that I was going to administer my own EpiPen in the bathroom. I didn't know if this would stop my reaction - last time, I needed an ambulance and two rounds of epinephrine to stop my throat from shutting.

For two hours I sat on the ground of the bathroom floor, struggling to breathe and jittering from the shot of epinephrine, as I went in and out of consciousness. It was truly my worst nightmare. I was traveling alone, and I was completely unmonitored for a full 2 hours after one initial check after I had administered the EpiPen. The flight attendants seemed bewildered and unsure what to do the entire time.

I came away from that flight stronger. I was adamant that this should never happen to anyone again: so I became an advocate for the necessity of auto-injectors on planes. I started a Change.org petition that had almost 200,000 signatures and advocated for the issue in the media. I am currently working with Senator Tammy Duckworth's office on the effort. My campaign has been featured on NBC Chicago, The Hill, Forbes, and the Boston Globe.

I've learned, the hard way, that I need to be better prepared for flights. I won't be trying any new restaurants, and I will be packing my own food before a flight. But just like I need to elevate my precautions as a food-allergic patient, the Federal Aviation Administration needs to step up their protocol and regulation requirements as well. Currently, epinephrine auto-injectors are not federally required to be carried, and the vials of epinephrine can only be injected by a medically licensed professional. All flight attendants need more intensive training on allergic reactions; all airplanes must require an epinephrine autoinjector on board; and, new regulations for restaurants in airports should also be considered.

My story is much more than a customer complaint: it is an urgent demand for national change. 40 million Americans have severe food allergies, and many more Americans do not know that they have one yet. Together, we are on a mission to save lives.

Let's continue to raise our voices and fight for our families.

About the Author of Converting Adversity into Political Action

Alexa Jordan

Alexa Jordan is a government and economics major at Harvard University. She is currently a junior elected to the Harvard Student Government, the Director of Communications of Institute of Politics FSG, and the co-director and co-founder of the Harvard Leadership Institute for the FY Experience. She has been named as a John Harvard Scholar; she takes pride in her academics. Alexa is passionate about advocating for those with food allergies, and she has had a severe tree nut allergy since she was three years old.

Positives of Food Allergies

Andrea Schmidt

Whilst many people might think that my food allergies are challenges that I face, I believe that have positively shaped my life in many ways. Although I would love to have a cure for my allergies (and especially to not have my cumin and dairy allergies, which for me are the most challenging), I would not want to change my past experiences with allergies. Here are a few positives of having food allergies that I would like those without food allergies to try and understand and those with food allergies to reflect on:

1. Food isn't everything! People with allergies, especially children, often feel left out when they cannot eat certain food at an event or restaurant. This is completely valid and sometimes I feel this way too. However, it has also helped me realize that my purpose of being there isn't for the food. I think people without allergies can sometimes overemphasize the importance of having the perfect food or drinks at an event. Sure, the food aspect is enjoyable, but it isn't what really matters. At a baseball game, enjoy the baseball. At a family reunion, enjoy time with your family. At a restaurant with friends, enjoy time with your friends. Of course, it is always amazing when family, friends, or restaurants ensure I have safe food, but if that does not happen, I try to focus on the real purpose of why I am at an event. Traveling can be especially difficult. A huge part of going on vacation for most people is going out to eat, but vacation for me usually means soy nut butter and jelly sandwiches every day. This contrast is particularly apparent when traveling with friends. However, I recognize I am lucky to be able to see new places and spend time with my friends. Even if I can't eat the food, there are so many other experiences to enjoy.

Tower in London

2. I appreciate when I can have food! People without dietary restrictions almost always take for granted the fact that they can go to a restaurant and order whatever they want, buy anything at the grocery store without reading the label, share food with someone, and even kiss someone who hasn't brushed their teeth first. But for me, the first time I was able to order anything from a bakery was mind-blowing. There were so many choices! I didn't even have to ask about cross-contamination because I knew that everything is safe! It was amazing! When I am able to eat at a restaurant, when someone cooks safe food for me, or any time that someone goes above and beyond for me, it is so much more of a special experience that I never take for granted.

Here's an example: my time studying abroad in London. While abroad, most students say they want to try out restaurants in the area. What did I want to try out? British grocery stores, a.k.a. my new favorite place ever. My first few times in the grocery store, I was so excited to discover new products. Who am I kidding, I was so excited *every* time I went to the grocery store! I must have looked ridiculous exclaiming "Oh my gosh, these veggie burgers actually label their spices!" and "Look at these coconut milk smoothies!" across the aisle to my friend, but I was way too happy to care. It never got boring. Would someone without dietary restrictions have *that* much fun discovering the wonders of a British grocery store? Probably not.

Ordering Ice Cream in Vacation

3. Trying new foods! Food allergies are often seen as restrictive, restrictive, restrictive. Yet my allergies encourage me to explore different cuisines and substitute different ingredients. Sure, sometimes I will try something new because it's my only safe option, but sometimes it actually works out. Tofu cheesecake? Delicious! Chickpea flour omelette? Yes!

   When I was diagnosed with a cumin allergy in 2019, it was my first new allergy since I was in elementary school. My diet had been similar for so long that it was a big adjustment for me. I was disappointed that I could not have many TexMex foods: premade burritos, refried beans, and many others. So many other foods were off-limits because of the generic "spices" label. Then, my friend who lives in Mexico told me that traditional Mexican food does not contain cumin and gave me a vegan Mexican cookbook for my birthday. Since then, I have tried so many new foods that I otherwise would probably not have tried. Even though I did not use cumin a lot before becoming allergic to it, my diagnosis forced me to think more about how I season my food, how to be more creative, and encouraged me to try new things.

4. My food allergies have encouraged me to learn how to bake and cook. Since I can't go to most restaurants and can't even buy many premade foods at the grocery store, my mom cooked a lot of meals from scratch for most of my life. When my brother and I were little, we often baked with her. I began baking on my own during high school and started cooking when I went to college. Because of my allergies I frequently have to make substitutions in recipes, which has taught me to be creative in the kitchen. I almost always modify or add ingredients that I don't have to, and I have even created my own recipes.

Every year for Christmas, my mom, brother, and I bake gingerbread cookies!

5. Nutrition! A lot of people without allergies think my allergies help me be healthier, which I would say is sometimes true. Nowadays stores sell many allergy-friendly foods (some of which are unhealthy), so reading labels encourages me to think about what is in the food I eat. Additionally, homemade food is typically healthier than going out to eat or buying premade processed foods. Learning about how to make substitutions in recipes can also lead to not only allergy-friendly modifications, but healthy modifications as well.

6. Food allergies teach you to speak up for yourself. With allergies, in order to be safe you *have* to communicate your needs. This can be very difficult, especially for an introvert like me, but it is a useful life skill that can be applied to other situations as well. If you're used to saying no when people offer you food, it's a lot easier to overcome peer pressure, when it comes to things like drugs or alcohol.

7. Food allergies also teach responsibility. Always carrying my Epi-Pen, checking labels, and transitioning to managing my allergies as a teenager helped me become more mature and responsible.

8. Allergies have helped me become more understanding of people with other needs and disabilities. People with food allergies know what it feels like to be left out, perceived as different, and sometimes even bullied or discriminated against. We become more accepting of people who are different than us, even if our particular situations and experiences are different. Since food allergies are an invisible disability, I am more cognizant of the fact that you can't always tell just from looking at someone what challenges they face. I also believe disability accommodations are extremely important, even if they are different from mine. We need to appreciate and learn from each other's differences – it's ok to be different!

9. Food allergies provide a sense of community and mutual understanding. Since food allergies are less common in my age group than they are for children and teenagers now, I rarely met other kids with food allergies

> when growing up. Until I went to the FARE Teen Summit in 2016, I had never met anyone who had as many allergies as I do. Meeting other people with allergies is an incredible experience because even though we start as strangers, on some level we are connected by our similar experiences. We don't need to explain our allergies to each other, because we already understand. Meeting people with allergies in person and online builds a strong sense of community that can provide mutual support and understanding.

Yes, having allergies sucks sometimes. I don't want to downplay the seriousness or challenges of allergies, but I also want to recognize how they have positively shaped my life. Yes, I would absolutely love to have a cure. But until then, I am going to appreciate the times when someone cooks safe food for me, when I discover new recipes, when I try more allergy-friendly restaurants, and as I continue to learn and grow not despite my allergies, but because of them.

About the Author of Positives of Food Allergies

Andrea Schmidt

Andrea Schmidt is 21 years old and from New Hampshire. She is a senior at Johns Hopkins University studying public health with a minor in environmental studies. She is severely allergic to dairy, eggs, peanuts, tree nuts, shellfish, kiwi, cumin, and seeds (sesame, chia, and poppy). Andrea was diagnosed with the first four allergies when she was six months old. Despite her allergies, she has been able to live in a dorm with roommates, eat in the college dining hall, travel with friends and family, and even study abroad in London. Her hobbies include baking, painting, and running. She has a younger brother who is allergic to dairy and eggs. She also has a Havanese dog named Rosie.

Speak up

Elise Buellesbach

Growing up I was always vocal about my food allergy needs, but it was not until I reached high school, I realized the potential impact of my singular voice.

I have always been interested in the United States government and the presidents, but it was my freshman year World History class, where I was learning about the Cold War, that I became intrigued with intergovernmental workings. My passion for understanding history and political interactions grew, as did my devotion to working to increase awareness and inclusion of the food allergy community. These two interests continued to grow, until one day they became almost one and the same. Every action sends a message; I realized that in order to see change in the world, my story, my experience with food allergies needed to be heard in the government and in the community around me. I quickly became more involved in the political actions that FARE runs. I learned to embrace my strong voice, using it to speak up and demand inclusion around me. My story is one of many, and while it is full of frustration and exclusion, it is also filled with strength and possibility. We all need to share our stories, as the power of a collective community voice is even more impactful than a singular voice.

Up until the end of my sophomore year in high school, I accepted the exclusion at school without protesting, because I had no idea what inclusion really felt like. However, with the power of a story in mind, I finally spoke up. As a person allergic to eggs, I could not cope with my classmate eating an egg burrito in the middle of class. Feeling unsafe, I spent the rest of my valuable class time watching from the door, trying to see the board from that awkward angle. I found it unacceptable that my learning was impacted in this way. I spent the summer emailing and meeting with the school administration, demanding that the school follow its own handbook policies that states students shall not eat in class. This seemingly simple request was not initially well received; however, the final arrangement created a safer space for all students with dietary restrictions.

After establishing an understanding with the school administration regarding the severity of allergies and the need for safety within the classroom, I addressed the issue of school-wide food-based events. Twice a year, the school has large celebrations with donuts served in the middle of the day to the entire student body. On top of being left out of these so called 'inclusive' and 'bonding' events, I was not at all comfortable with sitting in the gym with 800 students, their donuts, and their sticky hands. At first, the administration refused my request to eliminate the food, insisting that these food customs were tradition at the school. However, through perseverance and a series of correspondence, they heard me out. When this event rolled around in my junior year, I had doubt that my safety was a priority. However, when the food was served, it was popcorn! Pre-packaged, adequately labeled popcorn with two ingredients. No donuts! I am still amazed to this day. Change is difficult, and it takes a great deal of thought, energy, and effort to enact change. Creating small instances of change is possible through sharing your story.

The government has the tools of systemic change to affect the entire population. While I am not yet old enough to vote, I am absolutely old enough to demand change, and to be heard by my government. In September of 2019, I had the opportunity to meet with my Representative in Congress to discuss co-sponsoring the FASTER Act (H.R. 2117) and (S. 3451). Congresswoman Anna Eshoo (D-CA-18) is the chair of the Subcommittee of Health in the House of Representatives. In order to achieve a full House vote on the bill, it must go through the Subcommittee of Health, making her support of this bill crucial. Talking with a member of Congress seemed daunting, when in reality I got an opportunity to share my story and express the sheer importance of increasing the labeling laws in the United States. Due to Congresswoman Eshoo's position as the Chair of the Subcommittee on Health, she did not co-sponsor the bill, however, she did express her support of the food allergy community. My story is directly influencing federal legislation. That is the power of one story.

Advocating, creating change, and speaking out, are not easy tasks. However, I am driven by the exclusion I have experienced from my food allergies. I fight for a more inclusive and safer environment. I have plenty of experience sitting at my own table, bringing my own food, avoiding social events because of food; and, while each individual moment is filled with frustration, the overall experience has filled me with strength and determination to seek change. Hiding in fear of having food allergies is admittedly easier. However, using my story to make the world a better place fills me with hope, reminding me that every story matters. Sharing my story, whether in small everyday moments or at large government meetings, is how I can help create change. My power to create change comes from my story, which gives me a never-ending supply determination to see the world become a more inclusive place.

FARE
FARE SUMMIT 2019
Speaker
Ready Room

About the Author of Speak up

Elise Buellesbach

Elise Buellesbach is a senior at Presentation High School in California. She is allergic to eggs, chicken, and turkey and has Celiac Disease. She is not hindered by her food restrictions but is empowered to be a voice for change. Elise is a fierce advocate for inclusion, having worked with both FARE and members of Congress to usher in more substantial food allergy legislation. When she is not working for change, Elise is a passionate swimmer who loves to be in the water.

Lessons Learned at the Park

Emily McElroy

The park was always one of my favorite places when I was growing up: the slides were fun to race down, and the monkey bars were perfect for adventuring. But out of all the things to do at the park, the swing set was what I loved the most. I would always start swinging slowly and then push myself higher and higher into the clouds until I felt like I was flying. Something about swinging through the air was always so freeing.

One day, however, this all changed. I was at one of my favorite parks in my neighborhood with some of the kids from my playgroup. They were off playing on the big slides whilst I was, of course, on the swing set. This day in particular was perfect for swinging: it was one of those perfect California September mornings, where the wind rustles through the trees and brings a light breeze. That afternoon, I was swinging by myself when another girl I had seen around the park came by. I put my feet into the tan bark and slowly came to a halt. She came over and joined me on the swing set and we began talking. She was super friendly and asked me if I wanted to share a snack with her. She pulled out a bag of different shapes of pretzels that I had never seen before. Without thinking, I reached into her snack bag, pulled out a round and puffy pretzel ball, and slowly bit into it.

Immediately, I knew something was wrong. The pretzel was softer than any I had tried before and left a sour, salty taste in my mouth. I tried to spit out the remains but could feel the pretzel sticking to the back of my throat. My stomach dropped, and I could feel my mouth getting hot and dry. I ran away from the swing set and over to the picnic tables where my mom was sitting with some of the other moms. She took one look at my face and instantly knew what had happened.

We immediately left the park and went back to the car where my mom pulled out the yellow epi pen. I had used it before, but I had been much younger and the memories were fuzzy and unclear. My mom could tell I was extremely nervous and fearful about having to use my epi, but she calmly told me that she needed to give it to me right away for me to feel better. I clenched my fists tightly as she administered it, counting to ten out loud, and after it was over, we quickly drove to the hospital. I was pumping with adrenaline, but I realized the epi pen had made me feel better instantaneously: the tingling in my lips slowly subsided, and my throat felt a lot less scratchy. Once we arrived at the hospital, I was admitted into a room to monitor my symptoms. It was a long couple of hours, but my mom kept me distracted with some books that my dad brought. Turning the pages of the books while my mom read to me helped take my mind off of my reaction. Several hours passed and I showed no signs of symptoms, so I was allowed to leave the hospital and go home with my mom.

I was sluggish and exhausted from a combination of the Benadryl and the stress from that morning, but I was glad to be going home. As we walked out of the hospital, an ambulance pulled in, sirens blaring. A boy was pulled out on a stretcher, covered in red blotchy hives and accompanied by his mom. I was shocked when I recognized him: it was one of my friends from the park. His mom informed us that shortly after we left the park, he had eaten the same peanut butter-filled pretzels that I had. However, he didn't have an epi pen with him and was not given one until almost an hour after he had eaten the pretzels. While he ended up being fine, the delay in administering his epi pen caused his reaction to be significantly worse than mine, and he had to stay in the hospital for two days to recover.

After this experience, the park was still one of my favorite places to visit and the swing set always brought me joy. But I was always a lot more cautious at the park about my food allergies. I learned several lessons from this experience that I still use to this day, almost 15 years later!

#1: Don't accept snacks from anyone without asking first. Especially any in Ziploc bags without ingredient labels!

#2: Your epi pen is an amazing, life-saving device! It's not something that's scary. If you think you may be having a reaction, use it as soon as possible!

#3: Don't be afraid to embrace your food allergies. They are an important part of who you are and what makes you special.

About the Author of Lessons Learned at the Park

Emily McElroy

Emily McElroy is 20 years old and from the California Bay Area. She was born with a severe peanut allergy and has since developed allergies to several tree nuts, as well as an intolerance to gluten. She is currently a student at Scripps College, where she studies Public Policy and Economics and plays on the water polo team.

Food Allergies Made Me Who I Am

Alia O'Brien

Food allergies are hard, and I will always stand by that statement. They've hurt me, challenged me, caused me to be left out, and more. It is because of those experiences, however, that I am resilient, forward thinking, and inclusive. While growing up with food allergies is definitely difficult, it helped shape me as a person.

I know it sounds cheesy. I'm the first person to roll my eyes when someone talks about how their struggles don't define them or hold them back, or how they've shaped them into the person they are. However, when people discuss how their struggles don't define them, they usually leave out what I consider to be the most important part: the struggle itself.

My first distinct memory relating to my food allergies is from kindergarten. It was a day that we had a substitute teacher and we were doing a math activity that required Goldfish crackers (side note: why do so many math activities use food when you're little? Surely there has to be something else we could use. Pencils, stickers, erasers, anything. It's safer and more inclusive!). When the teacher came over to my table to pass out our Goldfish, I calmly explained to him that I was allergic to dairy and couldn't work with them. I had some safe cereal in a special container in the back of the room, and asked if I could use that instead. He said no and that I had to use Goldfish, because that was what the activity required. I remember being so scared. What if some cheese dust got into one of the cracks on my hand? What if I forgot and accidentally touched my face? What if I didn't wash my hands well enough and some cheese dust was left? I was terrified. I knew what could happen if I somehow ingested the cheese: I understood all too well that I could go into anaphylactic shock. I was an extremely obedient little kid though, terrified of getting into anything that might resemble trouble. So, I used the Goldfish.

According to my mom, when I got home from school that day, I didn't move my lips at all when I talked. I told her I was too scared that I had gotten cheese dust on them and that if I moved them the wrong way, the dust would get into my mouth and cause an allergic reaction. I don't really remember how she got me talking regularly again, but I do know what came next: one of the many talks that comes with being an allergic kid. My mom explained to me that if I am ever put in a situation like that again, I am allowed to say "I'm sorry, I cannot participate in this activity", and then respectfully sit out. She also said if there is ever a situation where I am scared for my safety, that I am allowed to leave. No matter if it was someone's house, or a classroom, I am allowed to get up and leave (respectfully) if I do not feel safe.

My little five-year-old brain exploded when she said that. Disobeying adults scared me, but defying someone in that drastic a manner? That sounded outrageous! My mom explained to me that it is okay to make sure my health isn't sacrificed. It's okay to stand up and say what I need to if it keeps me safe, and that if I'm being told to put myself in an unsafe position even after explaining why it's unsafe, I am allowed to leave. Of course, I had to do it respectfully, and I couldn't just hang out in the hallway. My destination was to the school nurse (who was amazing at the time) because she could make sure I was safe.

Thankfully, I was never put in a situation like that again, but there was one time when I did have to respectfully say no. My family moved across town the summer before fourth grade. It was a totally new school district with totally new people. This meant more people to teach about allergies, go over my 504 plan with, and explain my situation. My previous school had been amazing: not only did they always take us seriously, but they encouraged differences to be seen as normal. They encouraged us to talk about them, learn from them, and embrace them. It was an extremely supportive environment, and I flourished there. The staff at my new school, however, especially the nurse, were less than cooperative.

I remember the first time I went to the nurse's office to get Benadryl. My outdoor allergies were going haywire, and I wanted them to stop. The nurse's office was right inside the main administrative office, which meant that in order to get to it, I had to go past the secretary first. I walked in and told her I needed to get some Benadryl because my throat was itchy, and she asked me if I had used my epi pen. I was immediately nervous: I had never used my epi pen before, and I didn't think it was necessary for this situation. Before I knew what was happening, the secretary, principal, and vice principal were all there telling me I needed to use my epi pen and that they would call 911. I knew it wasn't necessary to use my epi pen, but they all believed it was. I tried to stay very calm and respectful while I explained that I only needed a Benadryl because my throat was itchy and that using my epi pen would be an overreaction. It took me somewhere between 3 and 5 minutes to convince them I did not need to use my epi pen, but they were still insistent upon calling 911. By the time the paramedics got there, I was shaking with anxiety. I was surrounded by panicking adults who thought I was having a deadly allergic reaction, even though it was just my throat itching, which was a common outdoor allergy symptom for me. I was picturing the paramedics hauling me away in a stretcher while I was screaming "no, I don't need to be taken to the hospital!" Thankfully, the paramedics that arrived that day were extremely kind. They were able to calm me down while doing the normal things like take my temperature, blood pressure, oxygen levels, and other basic medical assessments. By the time they were finished, my dad was there. The paramedics told everyone that I was fine, neither epinephrine nor a trip to the hospital were necessary. I remember being so relieved when they said that, because not only did it mean I was correct, it meant they weren't going to take me away on a stretcher. The school ended up letting my dad take me home for a little while so that I could calm down.

The reason I talk about this experience is not because I want pity. It's to point out how the experience from kindergarten gave me the ability to stand up and advocate for what I needed. If the Goldfish incident had never happened, if I had never been told that I was allowed to say no to adults, fourth grade me wouldn't have known she was allowed to say no. I would've ended up using my epi pen, and this story would have a completely different ending.

This story also highlights how quickly allergic kids have to grow up. At 8 years old, I already had to know how to advocate for myself. I understood that I knew more about my allergies and therefore I knew what I needed most of the time. I was able to say no to four adults I didn't know that well because I knew what was best for me. It was a very scary situation, but I knew I needed to remain calm and advocate for myself. That experience taught me how to stay calm, even when I am stressed, scared, or anxious. I'm now able to communicate to adults that I don't know very well, that I haven't met before, or that make me nervous.

I also have confidence in myself when it comes to dealing with my allergies. I knew that I didn't need my epi pen in that instance, and I was correct. Having the paramedics agree with me caused me to realize that I know myself best, and I usually know how best to handle my allergies.

My experiences with food allergies are not all about advocating, though that is a big part of it. There are also the normal, run-of-the-mill experiences of being left out of pizza parties, birthday parties, and classroom celebrations. One of my favorite stories to tell about this also took place when I was in fourth grade. While the teachers and staff adjusted to my 504 plan, a lot of unannounced food was brought into the classroom. Part of my 504 plan required the school to give us 24 hours notice of any food being brought into the classroom. However, this rule was broken so frequently that I started keeping a container of safe candy in my backpack, so whenever we had cupcakes for birthday parties, I wasn't completely excluded. As we approached winter break, the teachers decided to throw an impromptu mini holiday party for our class. Everyone was given a huge bakery cookie complete with green frosting and sprinkles, and a styrofoam cup full of hot chocolate (with marshmallows, of course). It was great, but I couldn't have any of it. We hadn't been given any notice, so I hadn't had the opportunity to make something similar to bring. So, I got out my fun-size pack of Skittles from my backpack and ate them. We were all piled into one classroom to watch a holiday themed movie, so I sat in the back with my best friend and quietly ate my Skittles.

This instance, I think, is when I started to get shy about eating in front of other people. Every kid just to fit in. That's usually the main goal: to be like everyone else. I always stood out at mealtimes, and eventually it started making me self-conscious. People would also comment on my food: how it looked like dog food, or smelled gross, or some other hurtful comment. Even some of my friends would make the occasional comment about it. It hurt a lot. In seventh grade, someone who I thought was becoming my friend came over to me at a pizza party, opened my box, announced how disgusting it looked, and promptly invited all of her friends to come see as well. That incident was the straw that broke the camel's back. I had been becoming progressively more self-conscious about eating my food, but now I was downright terrified to eat in front of others. I started hiding my food when I had to eat in front of others, whether it was holding my containers under the table or keeping it inside my lunchbox until I absolutely had to eat it. I would open my container long enough to get food out, then close it right back up so no one could smell it. I also started hiding behind my lunchbox every time I took a bite so that no one could see my food.

If I'm being perfectly honest, I didn't break my eating habit until last year. All the times people told me my food was disgusting, smelled weird, and made me feel like an outsider wore down on me. With the help of incredibly supportive friends (and an incredibly supportive therapist!), I managed to break that habit. Now, I do my absolute best to make sure other people are at ease. I find the person sitting alone and make sure they're okay and that they have someone to talk to. I go out of my way to make sure everything I do is inclusive. I don't ever want to put someone else through what I experienced. One of my best friends has celiac disease, which means she can't eat anything with gluten, so whenever we have a get together, I always make sure everyone can eat all the food. Our shared class has won doughnuts a couple times, and neither of us can eat them. When that happens, the teacher usually tells us what day he'll bring them in. The night before, I make cupcakes that are safe for her and me, so that we have a treat to enjoy together. I always do whatever I can to make sure everyone is included, no matter what. It's a huge part of my personality now, and it's a part of me that I'm proud of. Even though I struggled a lot to get to this point, I wouldn't change it, because I love how hard I try to make sure everyone is included.

One friend in particular helped me become more comfortable eating in front of people. Towards the end of seventh grade, I became really close with someone named Kori. They were the first person to ever ask what living with food allergies was like, and really listen to the answer. They seemed to care deeply about my experiences. When they realized I had never eaten at a friend's house before, they took me to the store so we could stock a basket of safe food for me at their house. I knew that whenever I went over there that in the corner of their panty there would always be safe food reserved specifically for when I came over. Kori also learned how to cook for me. When I talked about how my food was different, they listened with interest instead of disgust. Then, they invited me over so we could make pasta together. Eventually, I trusted Kori and their family with my food allergies so much that they took me on vacation with them once. If I didn't have my food allergies, I don't think we would have been such good friends. I'm thankful for Kori on a daily basis, and I'm grateful that my food allergies have given me an opportunity to get to know them so well.

One other person had a huge impact on me as well. I met her on the first day of fourth grade. I sat by myself at lunch, because I had to sit at the allergy table (which was separate from everyone else) and I didn't know anyone yet. I angled myself away from everyone, so that I could still see them, but didn't have to watch them or make eye contact. A teacher sat with me, either to keep me company or to keep an eye on me, and we made some awkward conversation, but I remember being lonely and wishing I had someone my age to sit with. About halfway through lunch, the girl who was sitting behind me noticed that I was sitting by myself. I had never met her, hadn't talked to her yet, and didn't even know her name. Once she realized that I was by myself, though, she immediately asked to sit with me. That made my entire day. The teacher sitting by me said no, because she wasn't sure about the allergy protocol and if it allowed people to sit with me or not. So I turned around in my seat some more, she turned around in hers, and we talked through the rest of the lunch period. I found out that her name was Addie (she wants me to mention that her middle name is Elizabeth), and that she was really funny. We quickly became best friends, and now, as seniors in high school, I still consider her a close friend. If I hadn't been sitting at that table, I don't know if I would have met her, and I am so glad I did. She's made me laugh, she’s been there for me, and she’s looked out for me since the first day I met her.

Growing up with food allergies was difficult, but the struggles I went through helped me become the person I am today. If that substitute teacher in kindergarten hadn't made me work with Goldfish, I wouldn't have been told that it was okay for me to speak up for myself. Even though telling so many adults that I didn't need to use an epi pen was scary, it taught me how to advocate for myself, a skill I still use to this day. Being made fun of for my food was awful and left me with pretty severe anxiety around eating, but now I go out of my way to make sure everyone around me feels included, safe, and loved. I've made some amazing friends who have helped me to feel more included than I ever thought I would be. I've had people go out of their way to make sure I am safe. Food allergies are hard, but because of them, I am strong, I am resilient; I am passionate, brave, and welcoming. I'm not grateful for my food allergies, but I am grateful for the ways they've helped me become the person I am today.

About the Author of Food Allergies Made Me Who I Am

Alia O'Brien

Alia O'Brien is a senior from Ohio. She is allergic to dairy, eggs, peanuts, tree nuts, kiwi, coconut, avocado, banana, and peas. She also avoids rice, oats, and chocolate. She's a proud band geek: Alia has played the flute since she was in sixth grade, and she has been in the marching band since her freshman year. This year she has the privilege of being the Drum Major! In her free time, she also enjoys reading and writing, as well as swimming and keeping active. She's also a part of the blog 'Food Allergic Teens', which is run by a bunch of teenagers all living with food allergies!

My Challenge

Arjin Claire

Every three minutes, an allergic reaction to food sends someone to the emergency room. I never thought I would be a poster child for this statistic.[1]

I am sixteen years old and I've been to the emergency room six times—that I can remember—all because of food allergies. To say that I've experienced my fair share of hospitals would be an understatement. But one trip stands out from the others as perhaps the scariest experience of my life: December 10, 2017.

During a busy afternoon at a family charity event, I was manning my craft table like I do each year. I found myself hungry, so I headed over to the snack table to check out the selection. Usually my family will make sure there is at least one item that I can have, so that's what I was looking for. This time, I decided to try out a KIND bar—something I'd never had before.

As someone who has been allergic to dairy, eggs, peanuts, and tree nuts for as long as I can remember, I'm always careful when it comes to foods I've never eaten before. I've been inspecting labels since I could read them to make sure a food item is safe for me to eat. Usually I double check with my mom or dad because even though I had "outgrown" my almond allergy, they're very cautious. I'm not exactly sure why in the moment, I decided to just go for it and not follow my usual protocol.

It is important to note here that I had recently outgrown my almond allergy

[1] Clark S, Espinola J, Rudders SA, Banerji, A, Camargo CA. Frequency of US emergency department visits for food-related acute allergic reactions. J Allergy Clin Immunol. 2011; 127(3):682-683.

and successfully challenged it, meaning I could now eat almonds without having an allergic reaction. Because of this, my mom was always pushing me to eat things with almonds in them so I could continue to build up my resistance. So I picked up a KIND Bar and read the label: "Salted Caramel and Dark Chocolate Almond."

Naturally, I thought I could eat it. If "almond" was written on the label, any other nuts it contained should be on the front as well, right?

After one small bite, I immediately knew something was wrong. My whole mouth started itching, and I proceeded to spit out the bite I took into the trash. I quickly read the ingredients on the back label, and to my horror, one of the first listed was cashews—one of my deadliest allergies. I started to freak out: I told myself that I would be fine because I had taken only one bite, that I hadn't swallowed, but I still wasn't quite sure what to do. So, I told my parents, and they freaked out even more than I did.

My dad and I picked up some Benadryl, a common way to suppress an allergic reaction, and I ended up taking nearly double the recommended dosage for someone my age and weight. In hindsight, this helped save my life.

Looking back on that day, I can't believe I didn't realize I was having a severe reaction. I had many of the symptoms that lead to life-threatening anaphylaxis: an itchy throat, slight swelling of lips, and an upset stomach. I spent the next hour and a half lying down in a car trying to rest and ease the pain of my stomach, getting up only to use the restroom. There was a part of me and my parents that believed since I hadn't swallowed the bite I took, I would be fine once the Benadryl got to work. Towards the end of the event, I even started to feel a bit better, and wasn't planning on going to the hospital. However, no matter how mild the symptoms, you should *always* go to the hospital if you have even an inkling that you are having an allergic reaction.

Thankfully my uncle, an internist, was present; he examined me and checked my heart rate. He recommended I go to the hospital as it's "better to be safe than sorry." Now, this motto defines my attitude toward my food allergies, but at the time, I didn't feel like spending hours in the ER.

Nevertheless, we went. Soon after I was admitted to the ER, I went into anaphylactic shock: I broke out in hives; it was hard to breathe; and, my lips were fully swollen. The doctors skipped administering an Epi-Pen in favor of two separate direct breathing treatments and a "cocktail of steroids" as the doctor put it. It felt as if my heart was going to beat out of my chest, and my entire body was shaking. My dad said I was experiencing an adrenaline rush, and it seemed like I could run ten miles in ten minutes. I recall trying to act brave for my parents, but my mom was crying, and guilt was written all over both of their faces. I remember the overwhelming fear I couldn't push aside. I remember thinking, "Am I going to die?"

I was being closely monitored by the ER staff when, about an hour later, my symptoms returned and I went into anaphylactic shock again, despite the steroids and breathing treatments I'd already undergone. I was able to recover a second time, but I'll never forget how it felt to sit on the hospital cot, jittery from the adrenaline and the needle that had to stay in the crook of my elbow, and to wonder if—despite the breathing treatments—my body would fail me. I had experienced allergic reactions in the past, but this was by far the worst. I was old enough to know what was happening to me and my body, and I didn't know if I was going to be walking out of the hospital that day.

They say hindsight is twenty-twenty. Nowadays, I can't imagine us even considering not going to the hospital at all. According to the doctors, I had a delayed reaction to the KIND bar, likely because I had taken a double dose of Benadryl, something that my parents and I had never heard of. I was well aware of how lucky I was to walk away from the experience. The doctors had advised that the correct course of action would have been to skip the Benadryl altogether and administer an epinephrine injection.

This ordeal epitomizes the phrase "lesson learned." I had never truly appreciated and understood what a life-threatening allergy meant, much less through firsthand experience. Now, I am extremely diligent with the food I put in my mouth—I practically study the ingredients, rereading until I'm certain I know what the food contains and may be cross contaminated with. Most of the time, I choose not to eat food at public events and family gatherings. This inevitably leads to questions and, I'm sure, some judgement from others. It took time for me to not care about wanting to fit in with others and to take my food allergies as seriously as I do now. An epinephrine injector is not a cure-all or a backup: it's a potentially life-saving line of defense. Having to administer it myself—stabbing my thigh with a large needle and holding it there for ten seconds—is a wake-up call unlike any other. It's the moment I realized the gravity of the situation, and that those ten seconds, which are incredibly short but feel like a lifetime, can mean the difference between life and death.

I have also come to understand that I'm pretty lucky when it comes to my food allergies. Don't get me wrong, I would much rather not have food allergies at all. But I am lucky. America's list of the eight most common food allergies, which are required to be labeled on all food packaging if present, include all four of mine—dairy, eggs, peanuts, and tree nuts (except almonds). This makes my life a bit easier, as long as I'm diligent about reading labels. And although my allergies are life-threatening, none are so bad that I can't be in the same room as them, as is the case for some people.

During my time as a Teen Advisory Group member with FARE, since 2018, I've had the pleasure of meeting some remarkable people who have experienced these challenges—their food allergies aren't included in the top eight, or they can't even be in the same room as their allergen. I have a tremendous amount of respect for them: their daily life, and many of the activities that others take for granted, are infinitely more difficult than mine.

I've also been fortunate enough to be able to challenge some of my allergies, as I mentioned earlier. For me, this process was a relatively organic one as I didn't participate in any type of oral immunotherapy for it. Instead, my allergist told me that because my almond and dairy allergies showed a dramatic decrease in severity through my blood and skin tests, I was able to challenge them to see if I was truly no longer allergic.

The challenge itself was one of the weirdest and most nerve-wracking experiences I've had, although I was safe in a doctor's office and had even been advised to do it. It was strange because I had never eaten almonds in my life, and then all of a sudden I was being told that I'm no longer allergic to them. In my mind, this was a direct contradiction to my way of life. What was I supposed to do? Just say, "Okay, thanks!" and start eating almonds after 16 years of treating them as poison?

To put it simply, I had no idea what to expect. But once the challenge began, I was instructed to eat a very tiny sliver of an almond. I then waited about 20 minutes to see if I had a reaction, and when I didn't feel any of the symptoms I'd become familiar with, we slowly increased the dosage. I kept doing this until I was able to eat two almonds, whole, without having an allergic reaction. In the end, I was successful—and I am now no longer allergic to almonds.

I went through this experience again with dairy, and I was successful after my second attempt in 2019. Similar to how I incorporated almonds into my diet, I've started trying to have milk and cheese—albeit in small quantities, as I don't actually enjoy it. But regardless of whether or not I'll ever voluntarily eat a grilled cheese sandwich or pasta with cream sauce, the best outcome of these challenges is the peace of mind they bring. I no longer need to think of dairy as a poison: instead, it's just a food I don't like.

As I've grown older, I've been astounded by how little people know and understand when it comes to food allergies, especially considering that over 32 million Americans suffer from them. I investigated this further and I realized that the phrase "lactose intolerant" has warped people's understanding of food allergies. When I used to tell someone about my dairy allergy, the first thing they'd say is "Oh, so you're lactose intolerant?" This misconception has skewed the severity of food allergies, and many don't fully realize the differences, which are fundamental at a biological level. A dairy allergy is in the immune system's wheelhouse, whereas lactose intolerance is nothing so serious—something that Lactaid can help out with. As soon as people ask if I'm lactose intolerant, many follow it up with "Can't you just take a pill and then eat dairy?" Nope. It doesn't work like that.

Living *with* my food allergies rather than *around* them is perhaps the biggest lesson I've learned thus far. Knowing that certain foods can kill you isn't a simple concept to grasp, especially as a child—*especially* when said food isn't dangerous to most other people and others don't know how seriously to take the issue. Most of my early years were spent dependent upon and managed by my parents, as it is for many children, and then gradually, the baton was passed on to me. My parents are always willing to help, but I definitely feel it's my responsibility to check the labels now.

My experience with food allergies has also been eased by my amazing group of friends, something not everyone with allergies has found. My friends and I are all comfortable enough to talk about my food allergies and even joke about them. If we ever run across a new food, someone will always say "Arjin is probably allergic to it." The humor isn't for everyone—gallows humor rarely is—but I know that when it comes down to it, all of my friends understand the gravity of the situation. The first time I ever ate cheese in front of them, they all freaked out because I hadn't told them I outgrew my allergy.

Though I'm still a teenager, I've learned my lesson well to take food allergies seriously and to take jokes with a grain of salt. Creating your "circle of trust" by surrounding yourself with people who truly, genuinely care about you and your well-being and keeping an attitude of constant vigilance may seem like grand prospects inapplicable to food allergies. Take it from someone who has wondered if the next moment is their last: these are absolutely integral to your lifestyle. Regardless of whether you have food allergies or not, chances are you know someone who does. Don't complain if they take a bit longer ordering at a restaurant. Try to remember to buy food they can eat if you're hosting. Give them the benefit of the doubt, and don't be afraid to ask them questions if you're curious—they just might introduce you to your new favorite food.

About the Author of My Challenge

Arjin Claire

Arjin Claire is a Junior at Sacramento Country Day School. An avid food allergy activist, Arjin has been a TAG Member since 2019. He loves supporting Liverpool Football Club and playing soccer for his local competitive team. He always seems to have a ball handy to either juggle or ready for a pick-up game. And if he's not with a ball at his feet that may be because his head is buried in a good book, or he's come up with some project and "experiment" of some kind because "he learned something new he needs to test". In addition, he also loves spending time with family and friends, playing video games, drawing, sleeping, going to theme parks, and occasionally buying clothes and shoes he doesn't always need.

Learning to Love My Poison

Himal Bamzai-Wokhlu

From a young age, I was told that certain foods were a major threat to my health. My skin and blood tests showed that I was severely allergic to a long list of foods. Peanuts, tree nuts, fish and various beans and legumes were all on the "DO NOT EAT" list. Antibody (IgE) blood testing suggested that many of these allergens would produce severe reactions, but my peanut and tree nut levels were astronomically high. I found out the hard way just how severe these reactions could be. I have had anaphylaxis several times, including symptoms like angioedema, hives, vomiting, face swelling, and breathing problems. Now as a teenager, I am a pro at self-administering epinephrine and my med-fanny pack has become my "signature look.""

Actually, anaphylaxis sucks. Sometimes it happens at home, but usually it happens when you are trying to have fun-- like when you are on vacation or out at a restaurant. The worst part about it is the first few minutes. You don't know how severe the reaction is going to be or if you are going to be able to control your symptoms. Inevitably, you worry about dying. One of my scariest reactions occurred on a plane from Hawaii to Minnesota. My mother had given me some peas to eat so she could safely feed me for the long flight home. My face started to swell, and I began to cough. This was the wrong place and time to discover *another* food allergy. My parents loaded me with medications, and pleaded with the airline staff to turn around the plane. We ended up grounded thousands of miles away from home, I was too scared to eat.

It took my family a few more years before they became to understand the gravity of my illness. It took years for them to give up eating at local buffets and start cooking at home. Sometimes my parents would argue about giving me an epinephrine; my mom was worried that the needle stick would traumatize me. Eventually, I was able to communicate to them that the pain of the needle stick was a small price to pay and that it was an important way to curb my symptoms.

A lot of people might think I've had a deprived childhood because of what I can't eat. Yes, it is awkward when I can't eat many foods at parties. It's inconvenient to have to bring my own food to events. Sometimes, I get hungry if the food plans don't go the way I want and I am away from home. Being Indian doesn't help, either: food is the glue in our social fabric, and nuts and legumes are a huge part of our diet. You walk into a social gathering and there are nuts everywhere; people are actually crushing nuts right in the middle of the party. It's also uncomfortable when your relatives or friends get offended when you can't eat what they offer. Sometimes, I can't even be in the same room, or I can't let their contaminated hands touch me. *They don't always understand.*

Many of my friends or family will say that they feel sorry for me, and I do appreciate their empathy. Having so many allergies is a pain, but I know that I could have much worse health problems. I decided to take advantage of my dietary limitations, and made the decision to be ultra-healthy. I learned how to cook my own foods and became a fan of elemental and nutritious eating: that means eating from the basic food groups without hidden ingredients. I can still make sweets but they are not a big part of my diet. I also decided to put my energies into fitness. I used to be big into gymnastics, but now I love to do pilates or any kind of workout. A big part of staying safe is having self-control and exercising good judgement. I try to stay balanced and maintain an even mind in all areas of my life. I also try to find ways to bond with friends that don't involve food-- like studying together or enjoying other situations like movies or working out. I have also found out that the people who really care for me won't get hung up about food.

About six years ago, my mother came across a therapy known as oral immunotherapy (OIT). This is basically a long-term desensitization process that involves eating a tiny amount of an allergen until you can build your resistance up to a manageable amount that would make exposure safe. The starting dose is infinitesimally small. I remember my first dose of a peanut, for example, was like less than a thousandth of a peanut because that is all my body could handle. It was at that time that I realized, "*Woah, I am really allergic*!" Typically, once you are tolerant from OIT, you have to eat that allergen multiple times a week for the rest of your life. Some people undergo OIT so they can eat the allergen in their daily life. Other people do OIT because they want to be "bite-proof", in order to avoid a life-threatening reaction from an unexpected exposure to allergen hidden in their food.

The first allergen I went through OIT for was eggs. The process of OIT had its challenges. First of all, the doctor was 3.5 hours away so we would have to leave at 5 in the morning and make a 600-mile round trip. I'd take a dose in the doctor's office, and then have to trial a new dose on my own for the next few weeks. Sometimes, it'd go without a hitch, but sometimes I'd have reactions. Also, there is a 2 to 2.5-hour restriction on exercise, or baths, or any meaningful activity after your dose, and some people have tended to react from their OIT at night. So, for the last five years, I have had to get up at 5:30 in the morning-- no exceptions. Finally, sometimes, even when I did my best, when I was in the process of updosing (or training my body to accept higher doses of the allergen), I would still react. Sometimes, I got Benadryl before school. Other times, due to an impending illness or being overly active, I would have reactions despite following all the dosing rules. I have had more than a few episodes where I've had to give myself epi or go to the hospital due to updosing OIT.

Despite this, I loved the freedom I got with OIT maintenance. After a few years, my body stabilized and I stopped reacting to eggs. I was able to eat baked goods; I was able to go to restaurants without the waiting staff getting annoyed at me for having so many questions about allergens; I was able to eat at more than 5 restaurants in my city. I went on to complete OIT for peanuts as well and to start OIT for some tree nuts. I found that I worried less about getting on planes. Previously, sometimes the nut dust in the air, especially when peanuts were served throughout the aircraft, would cause me to have asthma and mild allergic symptoms. We had been worried before about talking to airlines about precautions for my allergies because we had heard of allergic families getting kicked off planes. I was able to travel on transatlantic flights and even visit Ireland and Australia, countries we selected for being relatively safe from the standpoint of my allergies. I did have a reaction, though, in a restaurant in Australia. I realized that even with OIT, I am always at risk.

Unfortunately, when it came to managing my allergies, my luck took a turn for the worse last year. I had been on maintenance OIT for egg for five years, peanuts maintenance for three years and was in the process of updosing for a variety of tree nuts, when stuff started to go wrong for me. First, I developed *oral allergy syndrome* to lots of the healthy foods that I loved. I prided myself on elemental eating-- lots of raw veggies and fruits, but I found that I suddenly couldn't eat a lot of the foods that I loved, including cherries, cantaloupes, avocados, green beans, and more. The reactions were mild to moderate but restrictive and felt a little unpredictable as I was learning about my new intolerance.

Then, a few months ago, I developed severe reflux, which made it hard to eat without getting sick. We didn't know if I had developed some kind of gastrointestinal symptoms from my OIT, so we tried to scale the OIT nuts back, but I got sicker. My parents and I made the hard decision to stop OIT for tree nuts and peanuts after years of frequent office visits and breakthrough reactions, and out of pocket expenses to make myself safer. Because we stopped my nut OIT before I got any diagnostic procedures done, we weren't able to get concrete proof that the nuts caused the problem. Regardless, I decided to stay away from nut OIT for now: I will be severely allergic and need to practice strict avoidance. With the sheer number of allergies that I have now, I see this as a pretty daunting task as I start thinking about college and going away from home.

Nonetheless, I try to keep it all in perspective. I still have the healthy lifestyle habits that I have cultivated, and there are much worse health problems that a person could have. In addition, OIT was a very educational process for me. The tiny reactions and spectrum of situations like exercise or illness that could provoke reactions taught me a lot about myself and my body. When I had reactions, I learned when and how to administer epinephrine swiftly and without fear. Whilst I know that I cannot take risks with food, I savor trying new experiences and life's adventures that do not involve food - like ziplining and paddle boarding in sharky waters. Finally, I try to stay focused on what I want to do with my life and achieving my dreams and not to worry so much about what I can't eat.

Here I am (leftmost) after a reaction to egg. It can take a few days until the swelling from a reaction subsides.

The lack of dietary restrictions from OIT allowed our family to travel internationally for the first time. Here, we were at an underground mall in Sydney, Australia.

One of my vegan, elemental "charcuteries"

Even though I no longer compete in gymnastics, I love participating in pilates and yoga to retain my skills.

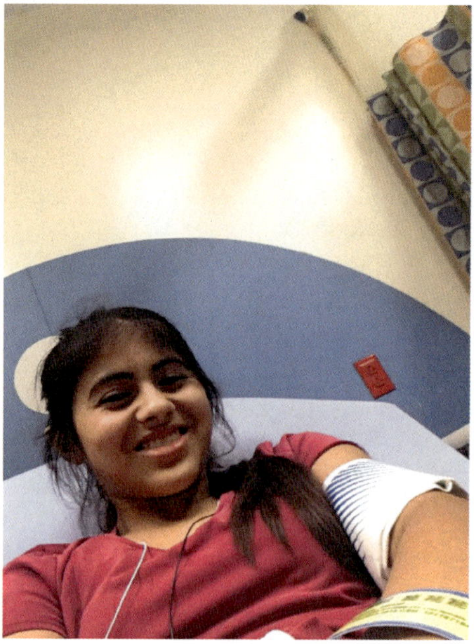

In the hospital after an anaphylactic reaction

About the Author of Learning to Love My Poison

Himal Bamzai-Wokhlu

Himal Bamzai-Workhlu is a high school sophomore from Gainesville, Florida. Since she was a baby, she has had allergies to eggs, nuts, and fish, and in later years, she has developed oral allergy syndrome for various fruits and vegetables. She aspires to learn more about the genetics behind allergies and immunology. In her free time, she enjoys freelance gymnastics, competitive math, and calligraphy! Himal hopes that sharing the story of how she has dealt with her food allergies will inspire other allergic teens to feel empowered to always prioritize their safety.

The Steps to Stand

Sophie Meade

Growing up with food allergies, I learned early on how to stand up for myself at school. However, as kids get older, food allergies make it harder to fit in, having something that singles us out from the rest of our peers. Teens want to be accepted, so having to say no to social events and food can be difficult. As a high school student, my food allergies impact my entire life, whether I like it or not. We always have to be ready, prepared to tackle the day-to-day challenges thrown our way for our safety. Simple things that come across as nonchalant could be anxiety provoking to a food allergy student.

A 'simple' class treat can quickly become something much more challenging, for example.

I was in French class on a Friday. Despite the prospect of the weekend that approached excitedly around the corner, a bittersweet mood hung in the air. Our wonderful student teacher whom we had all grown fondly attached to, Mademoiselle Rose, was leaving us.

"Can I have your attention?" Mlle Rose called cheerily. The end-of-eighth-period buzz died down. "Since today is my last day, I wanted to thank you guys for being such a good class, with a treat."

Uh oh, this can't be good, I speculated, thinking of my peanut and tree nut allergies.

"So, I made brownies!"

Since when did brownies appease high school students?! The last I had encountered this problem was in elementary school!

To my dismay, the cheers of my classmates answered me.

Let me take a pause. If you do not have food allergies, this is what your teacher announcing the presence of food feels like: imagine yourself in Paris; sitting at table, sipping tea, gazing down at the Seine River when all of a sudden the cafe owner springs up behind you, demanding you sing the national anthem in French.

That's what I felt like: ambushed.

I took a deep breath, reminding myself that these things happen. *It was no big deal, I could handle it.*

"Just so everyone is aware, these are nut free." Mlle Rose made meaningful eye contact with me.

I froze as my plans of quietly ignoring the commotion dissipated.

Disbelief coursed through me, and was only thickened by the fact that these were *homemade* (a warning to anyone with food allergies). I was taught to avoid accepting food from other households unless you knew for certain what ingredients they used, if they were good about cross contamination, etc. Personally, I had to see someone make it to believe it. It was easiest to just refuse, but now I was stuck.

I pretended to organize my flashcards while everyone gathered around the table, my mind racing. *What should I say? I have to be strong. Tell her you appreciate her efforts in making accommodations, but you just can't trust her. Too direct. Ask her when the last time she used nuts in her kitchen; has that pan ever been used? Argh, nooo! This isn't a birthday party. Plus, you can't just drill your student teacher in front of your whole class! I know, you'll just take one to go, and then throw it away when you get home.*

But then a possibility occurred to me: What if they *were* okay?

I realized I was the only one still sitting; I was going to have to make a move.

My hands shook as I slowly walked up to the table, avoiding eye contact with my satisfied classmates licking chocolate crumbs off their hands.

"Oh, Sophie!" Mlle Rose said carefully. "I made sure to keep the ingredients separate, and I even have the labels if you want to read them." She gestured towards the boxes set out on the table.

How can I say no to that?

As I haphazardly scanned the labels of the boxes, a cacophony of conflicting advice troubled me. I tried to sort out my thoughts. This was it, my two lives colliding. The high school student in me wanted to take a brownie, to fit in. I also knew that it was rare to encounter teachers who demonstrate this much awareness, so I wanted to express my appreciation! Should I trust her? I didn't know how to be assertive!

All the labels are fine; it's probably safe. I reached for a brownie. It must have been survival instincts that kicked in, because I suddenly pulled my hand away.

"Thank you so much for your efforts. But I would feel more comfortable skipping it, just to be on the safe side." As soon as I spoke these words, I felt an immense relief. I tentatively gauged my teacher's reaction.

But to my surprise, Mlle Rose told me she completely understood.

It wasn't until this moment that I realized I could show both sides of myself in high school. I was able to be true to myself by being kind and respectful, yet I also advocated for my needs in the process. I had to always be strong and stick to my gut, even if others didn't get it. Their reaction wasn't my fault, and I needed to stop worrying about it.

I walked back to my seat as my cheeks burned, under the eyes of all my classmates. I was embarrassed that I had to say no, yet I also felt a weight lifted from my shoulders. I still don't know what would have happened if I had eaten that brownie. They didn't appear to have nuts in them. Chances are, I would have been fine. Yet, I didn't see Mlle make them. I didn't know how much she knew about cross contamination. Those of us with food allergies, we can't afford to take chances. We have a responsibility to keep ourselves safe. Hard feelings can be smoothed over; people can be forgiven.

Our life, though, can't be replaced.

HIGH SCHOOL EXPECTATIONS PEER PRESSURE CHALLENGE STRENGTH CONFIDENT ADVOCACY
HIDING FEAR WORRY

About the Author of The Steps to Stand

Sophie Meade

Sophie Meade is a high school student involved in FARE's teen advisory group. She has been managing peanut and tree nut allergies ever since she was diagnosed with them at age 4. She presented at the 2019 FARE Innovation Tank, and has participated in multiple TAG projects. Aside from using her pen to educate others about food allergies, she can usually be found active on the tennis courts, or curled up with a good book and a jar of sun butter.

Experiences of a Student with a Food Allergy

Danielle Huli

Living with a food allergy is hard. It's more than just a slight inconvenience around food. You have to monitor almost every aspect of your life; and, you need to make sure you don't touch something that could have been exposed to your allergen. Once you're aware that your allergen is in the same room as you, you have to be even more cautious of what you do. Even when your allergy shouldn't be a big deal, it will still find a way to affect you. As someone who has a life-threatening peanut allergy, I've been forced to tiptoe around my life, avoiding peanuts, for as long as I could remember. Out of all the places I've been and all the situations I've been exposed to, handling my food allergy in school has been the most challenging.

I was forced to mature early because of my food allergy. In elementary school, I knew that I couldn't eat any food anyone else brought in and even had my own stash for when kids brought in birthday treats. At lunch, I was always aware of who was eating peanuts (usually in the form of uncrustable peanut butter and jelly sandwiches) and made sure to be careful around them later in the day. Sometimes, it seemed like I was more mature about my food allergy than my teachers. I remember one time, in fourth grade, my teacher brought in and ate peanut M&Ms most of the day because it was Valentine's Day. It was really scary, especially the fact that it took her almost the entire day to realize that she was eating peanut M&Ms in a room with two students who were deathly allergic to peanuts. I will never forget that day, and hopefully I never will. It's a wakeup call that no one, not even teachers, will truly understand and respect my allergy.

Middle school was actually more uneventful, in terms of my allergy, than elementary school. I have fewer memories of smelling peanut butter in the lunchroom and being scared that I touched something dangerous during those years. However, I do have some big memories that have shaped my reaction to my food allergy. One of the most prominent memories is in my math class in 7th grade. We were getting our tests back when my teacher walked up to me and whispered how she ate peanuts while grading the tests. After she apologized, I received my test and immediately thought how all of my school stuff will now be contaminated. I handled the paper with care as I maneuvered it into my folder, knowing that my fingers were now exposed to my poison, a terrifying thought. Another extremely revealing moment occurred during 8th grade health. We were put into groups and told that we were going to do a small advocacy project on a topic of our choice. I was ecstatic about this project because I knew it was finally my chance to raise awareness about food allergies in our school. I excitedly presented my idea to my group and they agreed to do it. However, I had to leave class early for a doctor's appointment, and when I joined my group at my next health class, they told me that they decided to change the topic of our project because they felt like food allergies wasn't an important enough topic. This was heartbreaking to me. The reason why food allergy awareness is necessary is the reason why I wasn't able to raise awareness. I was so excited to finally be more understood by the student body, but the fact that people don't understand the importance of food allergy awareness kept me from this.

At high school, students could eat virtually anything in almost every class as many students don't have a lunch period. This means that now, any surface could be contaminated with my poison. It took me about a year and a half for me to make this realization and become extremely anxious because of it. I saw students eating their peanut butter sandwiches (some in front of me even when they knew I'm allergic), and laying them on their desk or phone when they needed to use both hands. I began to be scared to touch any of my school supplies because of this. I began to feel the need to wash my hands every time I touch anything from school and every single time before I eat. I had never been this paranoid before. It got to the point where I could smell the peanut butter someone was eating during class (without knowing someone was eating it). More recently, this smell has made me nauseous. This was obviously a huge problem, but I was scared of telling people to stop eating their lunch because of me. This partially stemmed from the fact that I'm a shy person. However, the ongoing thought that people wouldn't understand and will therefore judge me for asking, was a huge factor in this lack of action. I remember one day, my health teacher announced we will each be presenting something to the class we hadn't learned yet and I excitedly chose food allergies. I told this to my friend, who responded by saying that I can't do everything about food allergies (we both had a science research class together where I decided to research the biological processes surrounding food allergies). This made me feel upset and insignificant. How could I talk too much about a topic that rules my entire life? How could people still not understand how important my allergy is? I still presented on food allergies, but this memory lingered in my head for the next year. It wasn't until the middle of Junior year when I decided that I deserve to feel safe in school and I began asking people to not eat peanuts around me.

Though I am still not done with high school, my food allergy already began to create problems with college. As I began my research, I came to see that a lot of colleges, especially "better" ones, don't have good protocols to help people with food allergies. Many colleges are amazing and have multiple allergen free dining stations, storage areas, and food preparation areas. However, there are some that don't have these options. Yes, they may show which foods have specific common allergens, but they base the safety of their students on the hope that cross contamination will not occur. That scares me. Even really prestigious colleges don't understand the steps that must be taken to ensure that their students are safe. What does that say about how kids living with life-threatening food allergies are viewed by these institutions? Are we really that unimportant that you can't spend even a small portion of your hundreds of thousands of dollars to make even one allergen free dining station that guarantees there will be no cross contamination? I really don't understand how schools could be so nonchalant about the lives of their students.

While these stories show the negativity I had to face due to my food allergy, there were also many positive experiences. For one, my time at school taught me how to be responsible and careful with my allergies: I learned how to approach people and ask them to respect my food allergy, which was a big step for my shy personality. I also feel like I did make my mark in some way at my school by doing so many essays and projects on my food allergy. One year, I even had my English teacher come up to me and say he didn't bring his usual peanut butter sandwich to school that day because of my essay on why peanut butter should be banned from schools.

Having a food allergy doesn't have to be a negative thing if you don't let the negatives get you down. I feel like this is an important skill to develop for the next stages of life, as people outside of middle or high school may not be as considerate about your food allergies. Middle school is supposed to prepare you for high school, and high school for college, and I found this especially to be true concerning my food allergies. The reason I decided to share my experiences is to give you an insight into what you may go through at school so that you are prepared once you get there. Hopefully, this will make your school experience much easier and safer. No matter what stage of life you're at, or how severe your allergies are, just know that you are not alone in your battle. Though it may not feel like it, there are many other kids, teens, and adults out there going through the same problems that you are. During my school years, I felt so alone. It wasn't until I joined FARE's Teen Advisory Group (TAG) that I realized how many other people are suffering like I am. If there is anything to learn from my experiences, it's that you will be misunderstood, and that's ok, as long as you educate people about your food allergy; and that you shouldn't be scared to ask others to respect your food allergy. If you ever feel scared to ask, think about it like this: which is more important, your life or their lunch?

About the Author of Experiences of a Student with a Food Allergy

Danielle Huli

Danielle Huli lives in Delmar, New York and is a senior in high school. She enjoys playing tennis and is captain of her school's varsity tennis team. Danielle suffers from a life-threatening peanut allergy. She hopes to be able to educate people about food allergies and help people with food allergies through FARE's TAG.

You Can Make a Change, No Matter What Your Age Is

Emily Sheridan

"I'm so glad I don't have a food allergy!"

I remember saying these words about a year before my first anaphylactic reaction. Funny how the tables can turn so quickly. For the first five years of my life, I didn't know I had any food allergies: I went around, eating whatever I wanted without worrying about having an allergic reaction. At that time, there were these two kids in my class with food allergies. Whenever someone brought food in for a party, they would eat their own snack. I always felt bad for them, and that's why I remember saying, 'I'm so glad I don't have a food allergy.'

But now, I am that kid. One night, I ate a single cashew. I did not like the taste of it at all, but that wasn't the only problem. Five minutes after eating it, my throat was the sorest it's ever been. Not only that, I was head to toe covered in hives, swollen, and I was wheezing.

My family and I didn't know what to do. We didn't know anyone in our family with severe food allergies, and we didn't have an Epi-pen. Because we also lived in a small town in Mississippi at the time, the hospital was not good. I was given Benadryl, and my mom watched me the whole night. When we went to the doctor the next day, the doctor gave me medicine to help the swelling go down, and told me that I had a nut allergy and to avoid all tree nuts and peanuts.

Immediately my life changed. I had to throw out my favorite snack that happened to be processed with tree nuts and peanuts; I now had to carry this thing called an "Epi-pen"; and, I felt like I could no longer be a normal kid. I had to learn how to check ingredients labels; learn how to stay safe with my new allergy; and, learn how to be ok with not being able to eat things that other kids could. The last one was, and still is, the hardest thing for me to accept: I'm still learning how to be ok with not being a part of the experience of eating food that other people can. I'm still learning to be ok with the fact that I can't eat delicious desserts just because I want to. I'm currently trying to learn that traveling to other countries definitely does not mean that I can always eat the traditional meals in that country. As someone with food allergies, you will never stop learning about how it will affect your life.

I never fully understood why. Why me, out of the other kids my age who can eat what they want? Why did I have to be the one excluded, the one that will always be different? I'd like to think that other people never thought of me as different for my food allergies. I did think this, until sixth grade. I was at another one of those events where they serve a cake that I couldn't eat. I was used to it by that age. Someone asked me why I didn't have any cake, and I said I couldn't because of my food allergy. They then taunted me with the cake and shoved it in my face. I let it go. I thought that would be the last time, but it wasn't. The next year, the same person taunted me about my food allergy by asking me if I wanted some tree nuts, and then they would proceed to put the tree nuts in my face; this happened every single day. I asked them to stop, but they wouldn't. Finally, they stopped, but I will always remember that feeling of being bullied for my food allergy.

I didn't want to deal with that for another year. I homeschooled for eighth grade. Now more than ever, I didn't understand why. I didn't understand why I had to be the one in three people with food allergies that has to deal with food allergy bullying. Why I couldn't go to parties at Starbucks because I'd have an allergic reaction to every food and drink there.

One day, I was doing an online math class. I took a break from it to search the web, and I ended up on the FARE website. I noticed for the first time that they have a teen section on their website. Intrigued, I clicked on it. I scrolled down through the sections: college, traveling, and something called Teen Advisory Group, also known as TAG. What's this? I found out that it was a group of teens with food allergies. I debated joining for months. I'd never known anyone that's been on the TAG, and I didn't know what to expect. On top of that, it seemed like you needed to have done something special for the food allergy community to get accepted into this prestigious group. On the last day they were accepting applications, I decided to try. I didn't know if I would get into it; if I did, I doubted I would like being involved in it. All of the questions on the application were intimidating. Have you been on TAG before? No. Do you have a website? No... am I supposed to? What have you done to help the food allergy community? I'm not sure... I mean, I've talked about it at school before? I tried to answer the questions as best as I could. I waited about a month, and then I got an email that I got in. Yay! I honestly didn't think that I would get in, but I guess that that just goes to show that if you never ask (or try, in my case), the answer will always be no. In the weeks that followed, I signed up for the projects I would be doing that year. As I scrolled through the projects that food allergic teens like me came up with, I realized that there are so many things I can be doing to help that don't involve having a Ph.D. or being a doctor. From setting up allergy friendly sections in food pantries, to writing blog posts and books, the projects people were coming up with truly opened my eyes to the possibility of being able to do something about my food allergies.

In the nine years that followed the diagnosis of my food allergies, I never thought I could do anything to help others with food allergies. I thought that the only people who could help were the allergists I went to for yearly allergy tests, or the researchers in labs that held Ph.Ds.; and, of course, both of those were nearly impossible to do at the age of fourteen and younger. But seeing the creativity that went into these projects really changed my mindset.

I started thinking about the change that I could make. One thing that I've always wanted to do was start a blog, and that's exactly what I did. I came up with the blog name 'nallergy', and got to work on making a difference. I spent months setting up the website and writing the first blog posts. When I launched it, all of the work was worth it. At the time that I'm writing this, it's been about a month since I've launched 'nallergy'. In just that one month, I've learned so much. There were things that I've learned that I never knew before about food allergies, and I'm learning about problems in the food allergy community that I never even knew about. Not only is my blog hopefully helping other people, it is teaching me so much about food allergies, myself, and the unbelievable impact you can have with just a little bit of creativity.

What I want you to take away from my story is that you can make a difference in any situation. You don't need to wait until you turn eighteen or until you have a Ph.D. All you need is a little bit of creativity and inspiration, and you can do anything. Another thing I want to encourage you to do is to take more risks. To me, applying to be a TAG member was risky because I didn't think I was qualified enough, and if I did get in, I didn't think I would enjoy it. But it ended up being one of the best decisions I've ever made.

Now, for some tips if you want to get involved in advocating for the food allergy community! Like I've been saying, creativity will be your best friend when it comes to this. You can turn almost any hobby into something that will help the food allergy community, one way or another.

If you would like to advocate from your couch, you can. I have been advocating for food allergic individuals from my own house during the Coronavirus pandemic. Here are some projects that you can do to advocate for food allergic individuals; and the best part is that you don't even have to leave your house.

You can:

- Have a live-streamed fundraiser for a food allergy organization
- Start a blog or social media account to raise awareness
- Write a book
- Create food allergy kits for younger kids to learn about food allergies
- Experiment with food allergy friendly recipes and share them
- Create an app

Again, this is just a starting point. The options for coming up with food allergy awareness projects are endless! I would also recommend following different food allergy accounts on social media platforms to see if there are problems in the food allergy community that you've never encountered; it might surprise you to see just how many problems go unnoticed right in our own community. We don't have to wait until we're older to make a difference in the food allergy community.

There are so many opportunities to make a change right in your own home. Remember: you are never too young to change the world.

About the Author of You Can Make a Change, No Matter What Your Age Is

Emily Sheridan

Emily Sheridan is allergic to tree nuts and peanuts. She has been a part of FARE's Teen Advisory Group since 2020, and she also runs the food allergy blog "nallergy." She hopes to make the world a better place for people with food allergies by advocating for food allergic individuals like herself. When she's not advocating for individuals with food allergies, you can find her traveling, baking, singing, playing piano and ukulele, reading, or coding.

From Discovery to Advocacy: My Egg-citing Food Allergy Adventure

Jacqueline See-Tho

My experience with food allergies began when I was just a baby. My mom gave me the tiniest piece, "booger-sized" (as she describes it) piece of egg and after consuming it, I immediately started to pull at my tongue. My lips and throat were swelling fast. My frantic mom rushed to give me Benadryl and take me to the doctor. From then on, I was diagnosed with food allergies to egg, milk, tree nuts, and peanuts. Although this wasn't a shock to my parents as my older brother is allergic to egg, milk, tree nuts, peanuts, soy, wheat, shellfish, and legumes, by the time it got to me, my parents were much better prepared and informed. Growing with food allergies I've faced many struggles and also many successes. To bring light to some of the hardships those with food allergies face I want to share my story, some pieces of advice, and provide insight on how food allergies have changed the perspective in which I view life.

I've grown up in an area where food allergy research is booming. From Stanford and Dr. Kari Nadeau to smaller food allergy clinics and research groups, Silicon Valley is home to cutting edge food allergy research and treatment. Along with parents in the medical field, I have been very lucky that allergy awareness is quite prevalent in my community. Food allergy safety requires vigilance and responsibility. My growth in these aspects has been very visible as it coincides with events in my life.

Most of my food allergy issues from preschool through elementary school were handled by my mom. She would fill out the forms, have meetings with the teachers, come by during snack time in preschool to watch over me, make all of my allergy-friendly lunches, gather my medications, and order my meals at restaurants. All things I would later learn to do on my own. My main duties at this time were to look out for myself and recognize when I was safe or unsafe. This meant watching out for what I was eating and touching, and what my classmates were consuming as well. During this time, I experienced my first memorable allergic reactions and I learned how to recognize a reaction, as well as how to get help and treatment. My time with allergies between the ages of three and ten was characterized by sitting at separate allergy-friendly tables, eating from my own special treat bag during birthday celebrations, and rejecting food and candy offers from friends. While I always had homemade lunches and never participated in bake sales, I ran into very few problems with food allergies as a child. Teachers were very gracious and understanding when it came to my needs, they looked out for me, respected my boundaries when I wasn't comfortable in a situation, and often tried to find alternatives in food-related activities. I had one teacher who would make a cake whenever someone had a birthday, and she made sure the recipes were allergy-friendly, so I could partake in the celebration too. This sort of stable and continuous support aided me in mastering the food allergy basics. My first big step in independently handling my food allergies came when I entered middle school.

The jump from fifth grade to sixth grade is quite big all around, with more homework, a larger campus, and more freedom. Adding food allergies to this list made life a little more complicated. I was now in charge of carrying my own medicines and not many of my teachers were aware I had food allergies unless I brought it up. With all of these new opportunities, there were also greater chances of me having an allergic reaction. My environment wasn't as closely monitored, so I had to be extra vigilant. Middle school brought some tough challenges like taking Home Economics and having to arrange special substitutes (which some of my group members found disgusting) when we cooked, not getting to participate in certain science labs involving eggs, to figuring out alternative activities to do with friends besides eating. However, I never let allergies define who I was or could be. Even if it was hard to take school cooking classes, I found one of my passions for baking at home. To this day, I love trying new recipes and figuring out ways to make food allergy-friendly.

In middle school, I had some really big steps forward in my food allergy journey. I had a school trip to Disneyland and my parents did not chaperone (although they did come along separately so that they weren't super far away). I was completely in charge of my own food and medicines. My parents helped me plan and make meals that I would need to warm up in the hotel kitchen, and we also researched foods I could eat at Disneyland. Overall, it was a great trip and my friends and teachers were very kind and respectful of my allergies. While I did run into a small hiccup when a waitress did not take my allergies seriously, it was a huge moment of learning how to order food and advocate for myself. I have often struggled with feeling like a burden to a restaurant or like it was somehow my fault that I would get an allergic reaction. However, I have come to realize that I need to be assertive and make sure that people understand how life-threatening food allergies can be and how I put my life and trust in a chef's hands. While you can't have complete control over a restaurant's kitchen, the best thing you can do is be clear and make sure you are prepared for anything.

I also embarked on a new path in 2017, oral immunotherapy (OIT). I began a multi-food OIT trial using Xolair at the Sean N. Parker Research Center, and I was treated for eggs, milk, walnuts, and cashews. Being treated for my allergies through OIT is one of my biggest allergy accomplishments because ingesting my own allergens on purpose had been an extreme fear of mine for years. I had turned down several OIT opportunities prior to that because I was so afraid, even though it would be under medical supervision and monitoring. The only reason I had agreed to doing this trial was because it did not involve any food challenges, which scared me the most, and my brother participated in it with me. My treatment began with shots of Xolair (known to help with asthma which I also have) and increasing doses of a protein powder of my allergens. This eventually translated into real food, while only a tiny amount, it was an unbelievable milestone to hit. After hours spent at the hospital, the work paid off, I completed those six months being able to eat one cashew, one walnut, three milliliters of egg white, and nine milliliters of milk. I continued on that daily maintenance dose for two years. I was now able to eat food that "may contain" allergens, which broadened my options greatly. It opened up my world, making it safer and allowing me to try new foods with less fear and anxiety.

For a while, my allergy journey was at a standstill. For almost a year, I continued on this low dose exposure of my allergens. I didn't see any problem with that as it protected me, but of course high school and fate worked in mysterious ways which led me to where I am today. In December of 2019, I did a presentation on food allergies for my English class on the facts vs. myths of food allergies. This issue is very important to me as I once had a traumatic allergic reaction when I was told a certain ice cream at a shop was dairy free, when it was actually only lactose-free, which is a common and deadly misconception. During my research, I came across FARE's website. It brought me to a whole new world and community full of other people like me! I discovered they had a program called the Teen Advisory Group and I decided I would apply in February.

This would bring me to my most recent chapter of my allergy story, food allergy advocacy. After being accepted into the amazing TAG team and meeting so many others around the nation who understand me and are just as dedicated to spreading awareness about food allergies as I am, I began to learn so much more about food allergies than I ever knew before. I joined seven projects ranging from allergy-friendly food taste testing, blog writing, recipe writing, school meal service research, helping start a nonprofit dedicated to allergy-friendly food accessibility, giving advice on sports and food allergies, to this very book that you are reading. I am so lucky to have found this community and to be a part of it! I really love helping people in this way, and passing on what I know and getting to learn from others. I really urge you to find ways to support the millions around the world that are facing food allergies and their struggles every day.

Also, in January of 2020, I began OIT again. Now at a different allergy clinic, I finally faced one of my greatest fears head on, food challenges. I have come out of it confident and successful! Food challenges involve testing tolerance levels by ingesting an allergen in increasing amounts over a short period of time until a reaction occurs. I have already passed baked eggs, baked milk, and most recently an entire egg! I have others, like hazelnut, peanut, milk still to come. I consider eating one whole egg to be one of my greatest accomplishments so far as it took a lot of courage and perseverance to get here. I never thought I would be able to do it. It has been life-changing! I will always proudly identify as a person with food allergies because no one should ever be ashamed of having them. I have faced some of the scariest moments of my life because of food allergies, but I've also had so many exciting opportunities and joyful moments. I have come a long way from that small baby who ate a tiny piece of egg, and I know there is a lot more to come.

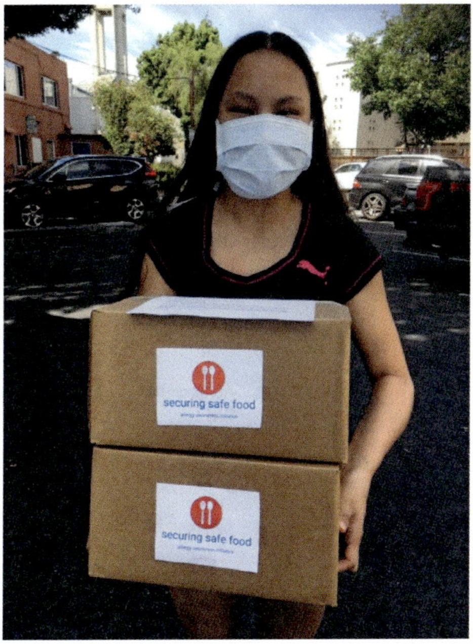
securing safe food
securing safe food

About the Author of From Discovery to Advocacy: My Egg-citing Food Allergy Adventure

Jacqueline See-Tho

Jacqueline See-Tho is a 15-year-old sophomore at Gunn High School in Palo Alto, California. She has lived with food allergies to eggs, milk, tree nuts, and peanuts her entire life. She is Filipino, Malaysian-Chinese, and German. Growing up in an area that is booming with research regarding allergies has made her very lucky. About three years ago, she was fortunate enough to become part of a clinical trial, a multi-food OIT program that used Xolair. She did this with my older brother who also has severe food allergies. As she continues to undergo treatment, her food world has opened up and she now feels more comfortable with the food that she encounters. She loves to cook, bake, and test new recipes. Learning how to make good food with allergies is essential. Some of her other passions include traveling, dance (she does ballet and contemporary), singing (she's in her school choir), and acting (she takes theatre classes at school and participates in shows). In her free time, she likes to listen to music, play with her dog (a Goldendoodle), read, and write. This is her first year being on FARE's Teen Advisory Group (2020), and she's really excited to be working alongside so many supportive, dedicated, and hardworking individuals. She hopes to provide some insight into what life is like with food allergies as well as some of the struggles she has faced and the accomplishments she has made! She is very grateful to her family and the food allergy community for supporting her!

Made in the USA
Monee, IL
20 March 2021

63337428R00045